My Shadow

Sheila Gore
Photographs by Fiona Pragoff

A & C Black · London

In this picture, how many shadows can you see?

2

When the sun goes in, what will happen to the shadows?

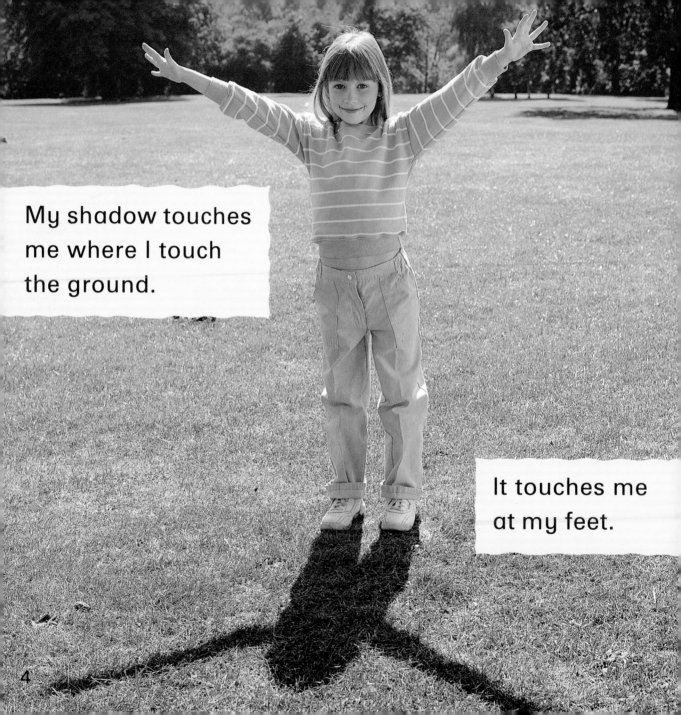

My shadow touches
me where I touch
the ground.

It touches me
at my feet.

4

It touches me at my head.

My shadow copies what I do.
When I swing on this bar,
so does my shadow.

If I jump in the air, what happens to my shadow?

My shadow is bigger than
my brother's shadow.
I'm taller than my brother.

8

When our hands are apart,
our shadows can still
hold hands.

When the sun is high in the sky, shadows are short.

When the sun is low in the sky, shadows are long.

11

With a bright light, we can make shadows.

If my hand is near the light, my shadow looks big and fuzzy.

Emma's hand is further away from the light.
Her shadow is smaller.

The small shadow is clearer than the big shadow.

Here the light
is shining on
one side of me.

16

Now the light is shining right behind me.

When Emma moves the light, my shadow moves too. It moves to one side of me.

Can you guess where
the light is now?

We are wearing
different colours
but our shadows
are the same colour.

The shadow of my hands looks like a butterfly.

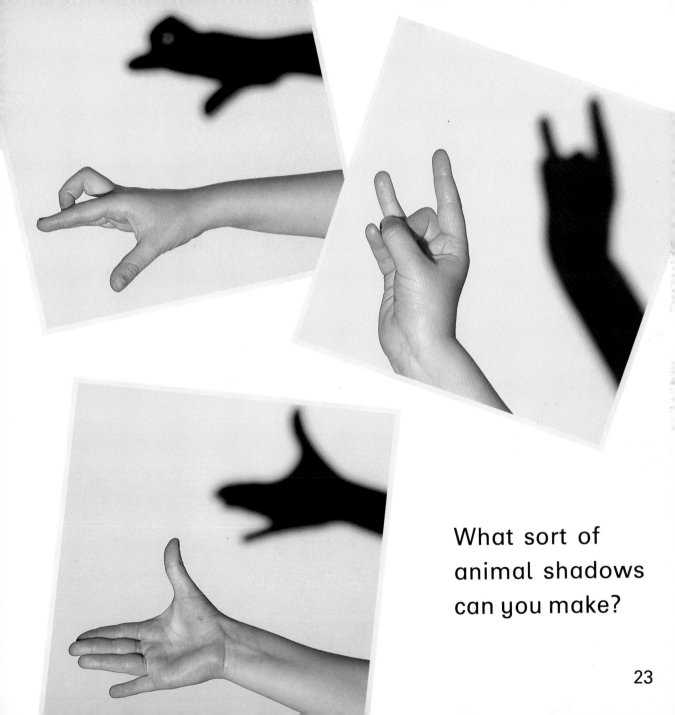

What sort of animal shadows can you make?

More things to do

1. Make a sundial
The shadows on a sundial help us tell the time. To make a simple sundial, stand a pencil in the top of a cotton reel and glue the cotton reel on to a piece of white paper. Leave the sundial out of doors on a sunny day and mark where the shadow of the pencil falls every hour. Write the time against each mark. Now, on a sunny day, you can tell the time from the position of the shadow.

2. Shadow games
To play 'Catch the shadow', chase a friend for a little while and then shout "Stop". When you are both standing still, try and touch your friend's shadow with your foot. If you succeed, it's your friend's turn to try and catch your shadow.

3. Shadow plays
Hang up a big white sheet and ask the audience to sit in front of the sheet. Put a bright light a little way behind the sheet and hold your hands or other parts of your body in front of the light to make shadows of people or animals. Try making shadow puppets by cutting out cardboard shapes and gluing them on to thin sticks. Before you start, make up a story which includes lots of different shadow shapes.

4. Shadows in space
Eclipses happen when the moon or the earth block out light from the sun and cast huge shadows in space. See if you can find out more about eclipses.

Find the page

This list shows you where to find some of the ideas in this book.

Notes for parents and teachers

As you share this book with young children, these notes will help you to explain the scientific concepts behind the different activities.

Pages 2, 3   All sorts of shadows
Light travels in straight lines and cannot bend round corners. So, if an object blocks out a source of light, a dark area forms behind the object. This is a shadow.

Pages 4, 5, 6, 7   Can you lose your shadow?
Shadows are attached to the object that makes them and make the same movements.

Pages 8, 10, 11, 13, 14, 15
Big and small shadows
The size of a shadow depends partly on the size of the object and partly on how near the object is to the source of light. When the child's hand is near the light, it blocks out a lot of light, so the shadow is large. When her hand is further away from the light, it blocks out less light and the shadow is smaller.

On a sunny day, shadows out of doors are different lengths at different times of day because the angle of the sun's rays changes as the sun moves across the sky.

Page 9   Touching shadows
Shadows extend beyond the object that makes them.

Page 12   Making hand shadows
The best indoor shadows are made with a bright source of light which comes from a small point – a torch is ideal. You can improve the shadows made by a torch by covering the reflector or most of the front of the torch with black paper so there is only a small hole for the light to come through.

Pages 13, 15   Clear and fuzzy shadows
The sharpness of the edge of a shadow depends on the size of the light source and how near the object is to the light.

Pages 16, 17, 18, 19   Making shadows move
Shadows change their position and shape as the light moves with respect to the object. A shadow shows only the outline shape of an object; other details are lost.

Pages 20, 21   Shadows and colour
Even though we can't usually see any colour in ordinary light, it is made up of all the colours of the rainbow. The light we see is the light that is reflected from objects into our eyes. Since a shadow is an area without light, it has no colour.

Pages 22, 23   Animal shadows
As shadows show only the shape of objects, they can look very different from the objects themselves. We can make the shadows of our hands look like a variety of animal shadows. The shadows cast by ordinary objects in a bedroom at night can sometimes look very frightening.